Inner Landscapes

An Exploration in Abstract Expression

by Tulasi Zimmer

Inner Landscapes

ISBN-13: 978-0-9892411-3-7
ISBN-10: 0989241130

www.tulasizimmer.com
Email:tulasizimmer@hotmail.com

Give feedback on the book at:
http://tulasizimmer.com

CRYSTALMOON
PUBLISHING

Printed in U.S.A

FORWARD

"Inner Landscapes" reflects the internal imagery I experience and try to manifest through painting. The abstract approach appeals to my years of practice in spirituality and meditation. It's a journey into the unknown, without an external reference, and the exploration of my Self. Ultimately, it is a lesson of surrender and the letting go of results that I am learning through this creative process.

I don't have a subject in mind when I start a new painting. I begin by selecting a color palette to work with. I randomly paint large shapes over the entire canvas, using energetic brush strokes of transparent paint diluted with a painting medium. From there, I selectively enhance shapes that I find interesting, and sometimes merge several shapes into one. I continue by adding values of colors that will push and pull shapes in and out of the space and create a sense of movement. In some instances, I will apply thicker applications of paint that not only provide a sense of depth, but also create interesting textural qualities. I prefer to work with oil paint, because it is easier for me to blend colors and create value gradations. I try not to portray representational elements in my paintings, because I want the viewer to interpret their own meaning to my art work and enjoy the visual experience.

-Tulasi Zimmer

INNER LANDSCAPES

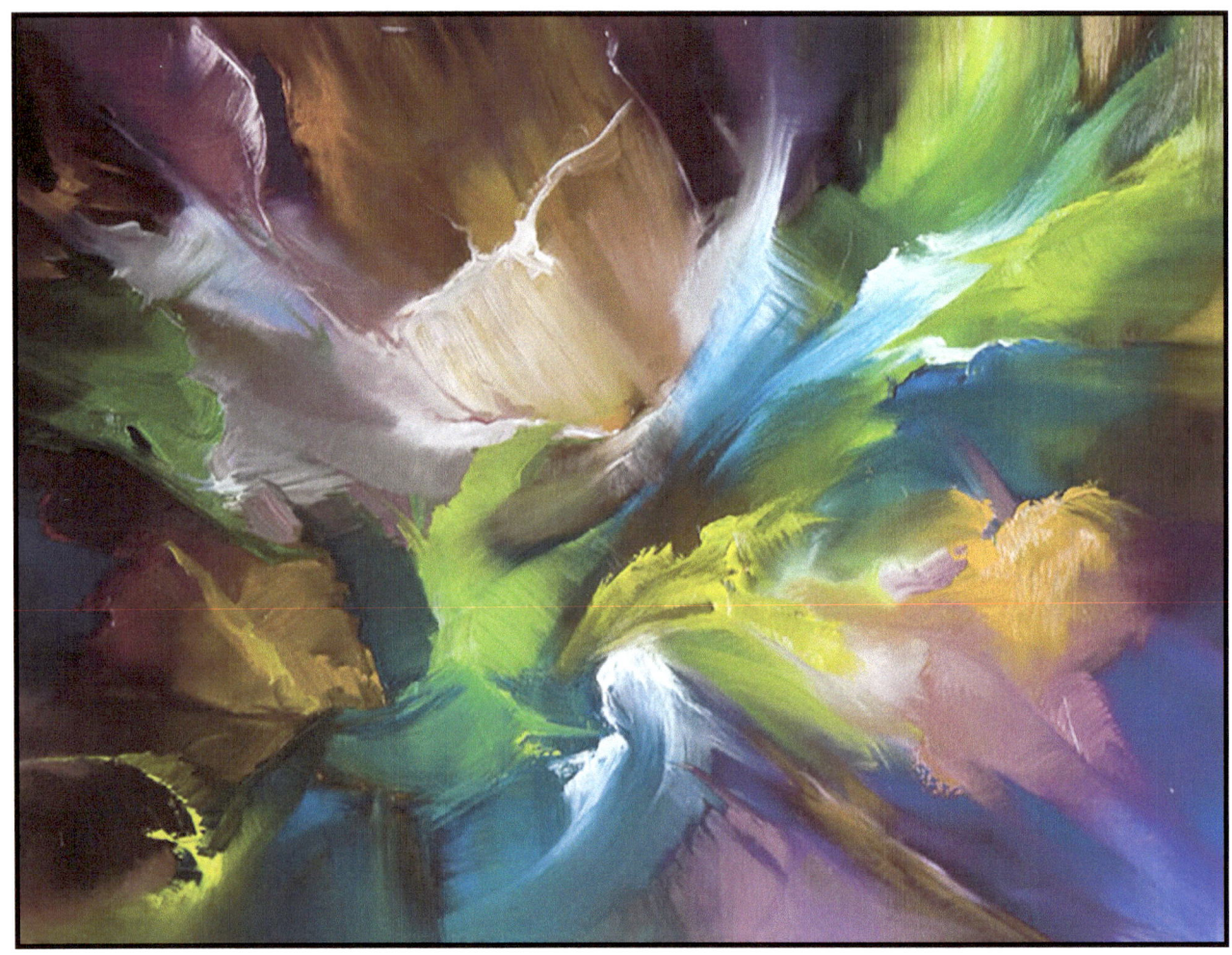

"New Start"
36" x 24" - Oil on Canvas
2011

"Logic will get you from A to B.
Imagination will take you everywhere."
-*Albert Einstein*

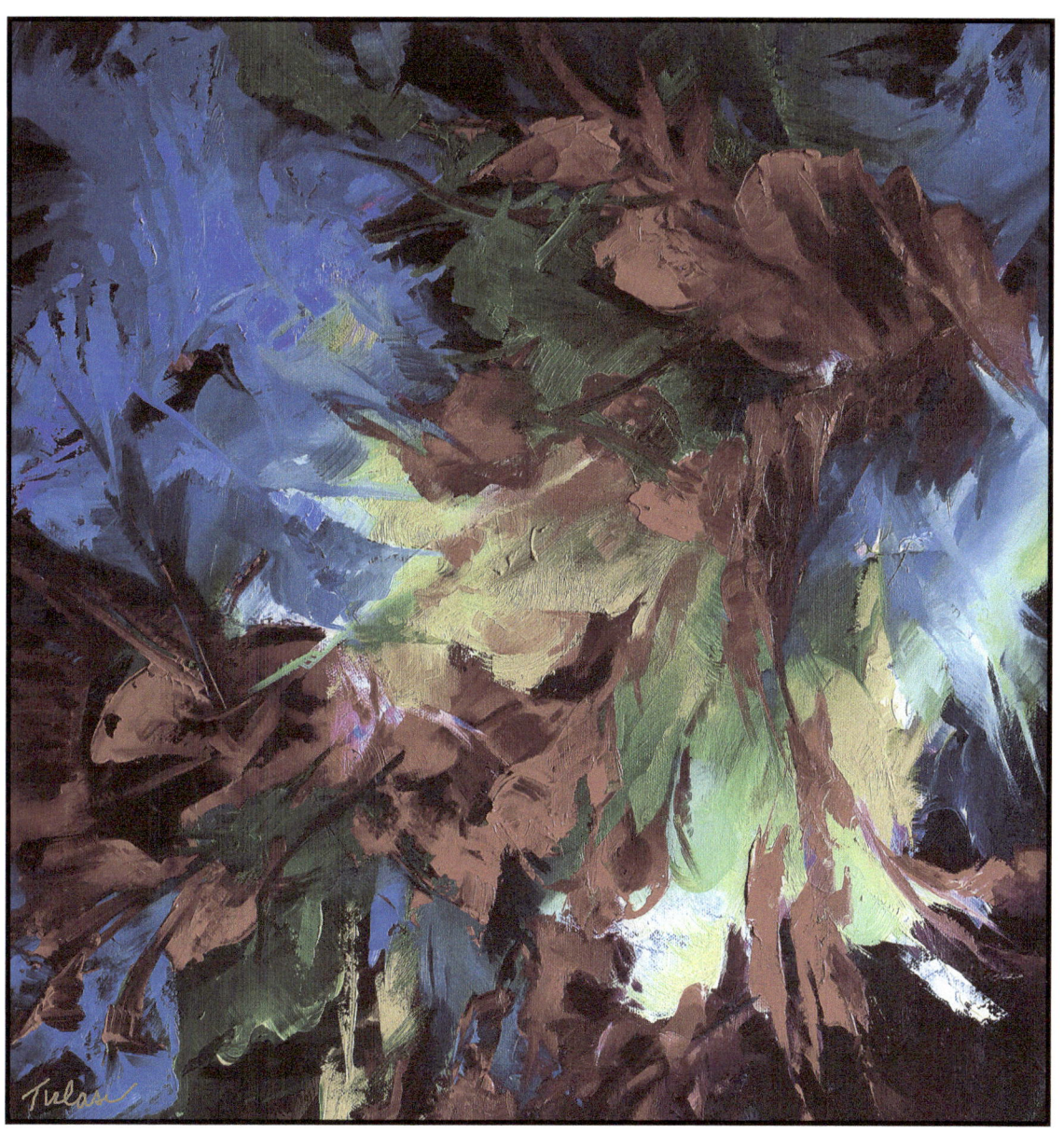

"Morning's Glory"
18" x 18" - Oil on Canvas
2011

INNER LANDSCAPES

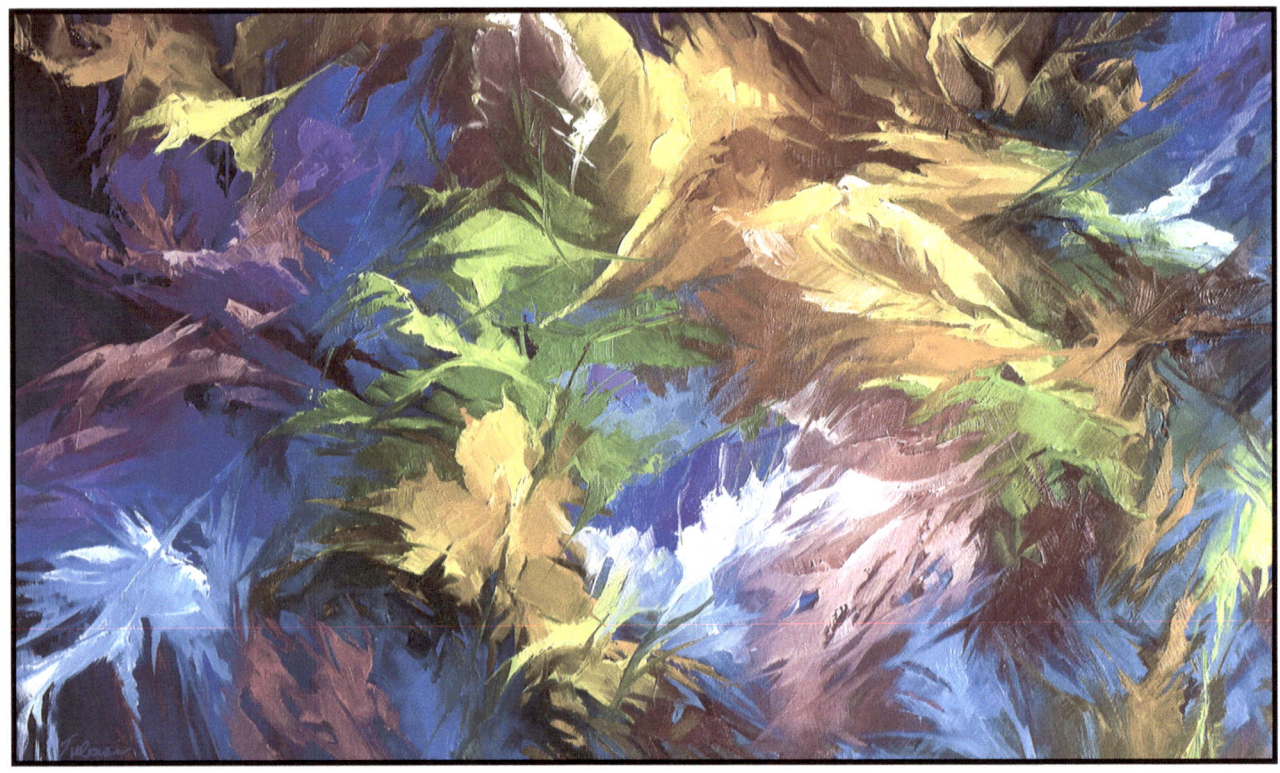

"In the Thick of It"
36" x 24" - Oil on Canvas
2011

"Our truest life is when we are in dreams awake."
-Henry David Thoreau

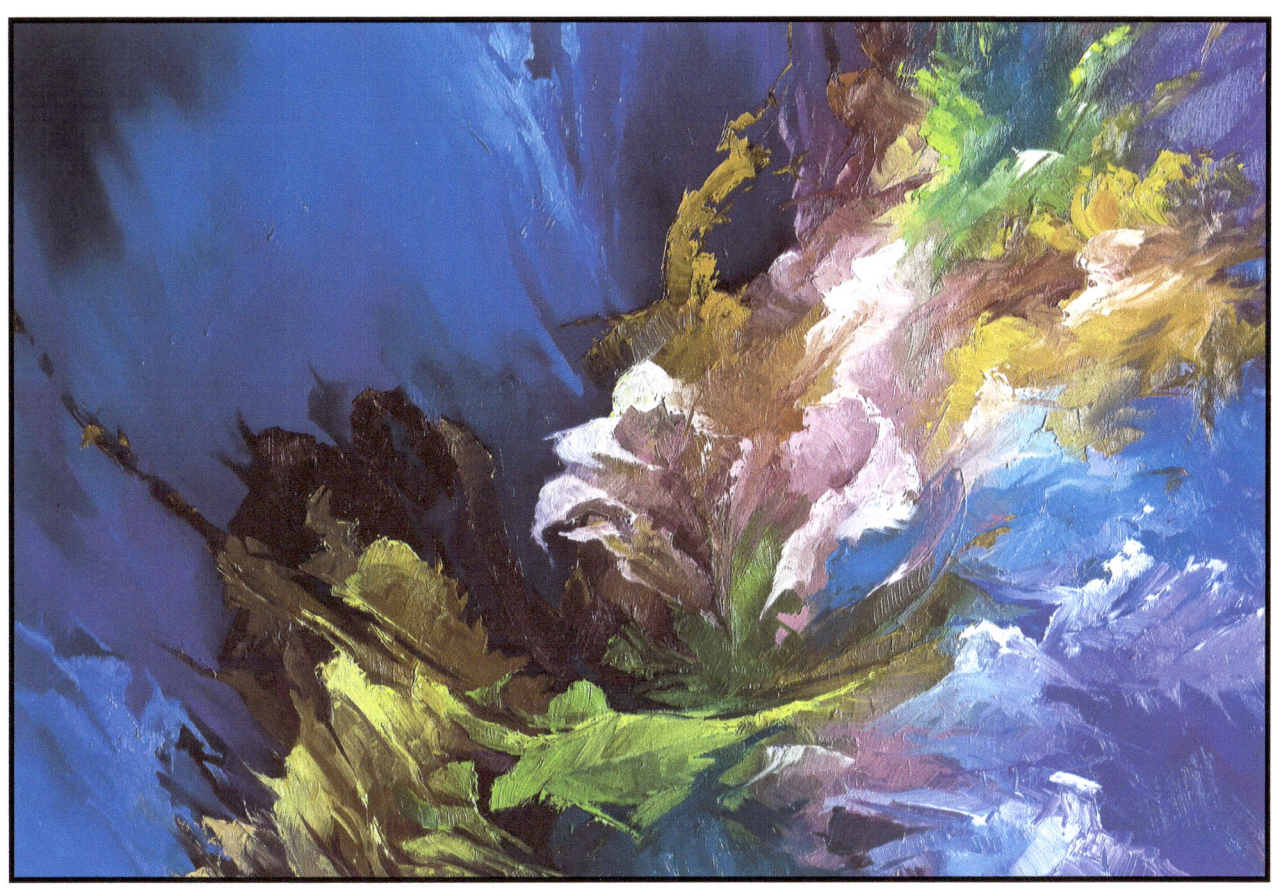

"Waterfall"
36" x 24" - Oil on Canvas
2010

"A painting that is well composed is half finished."
-Pierre Bonnard

INNER LANDSCAPES

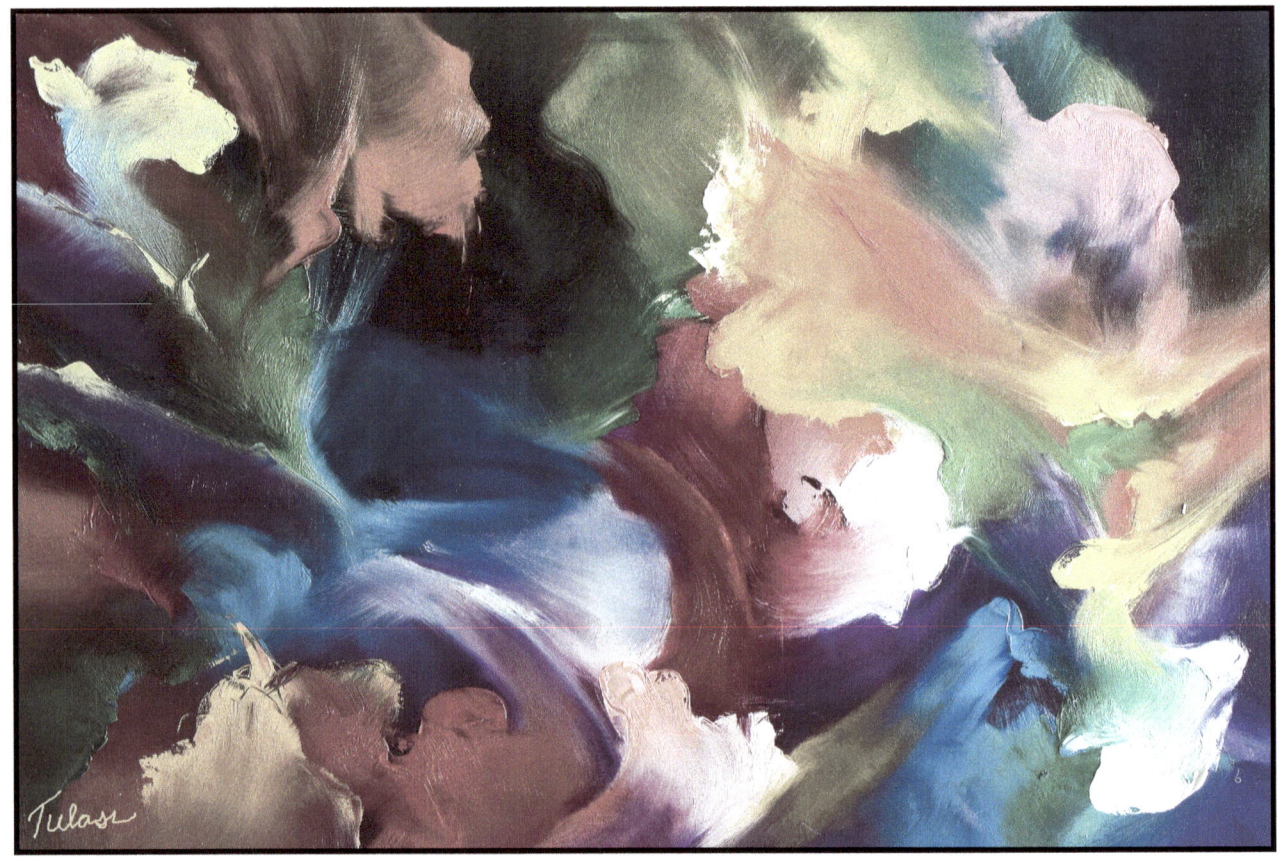

"Wonder"
36" x 24" - Oil on Canvas
2010

"Art enables us to find ourselves and
lose ourselves at the same time. "
Thomas Merton

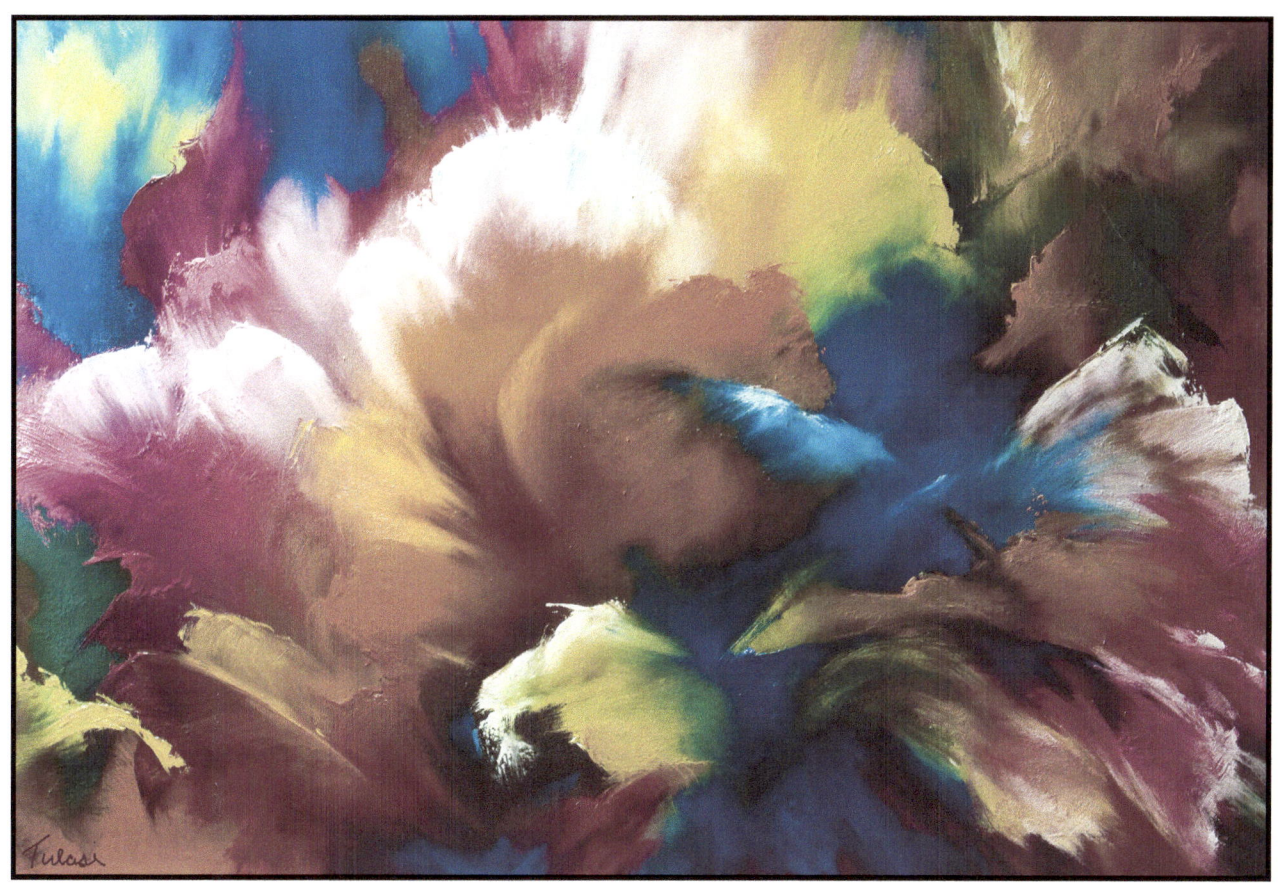

"Renewal"
36" x 24" - Oil on Canvas
2011

"The essence of all art is to
have pleasure in giving pleasure."
Dale Carnegie

INNER LANDSCAPES

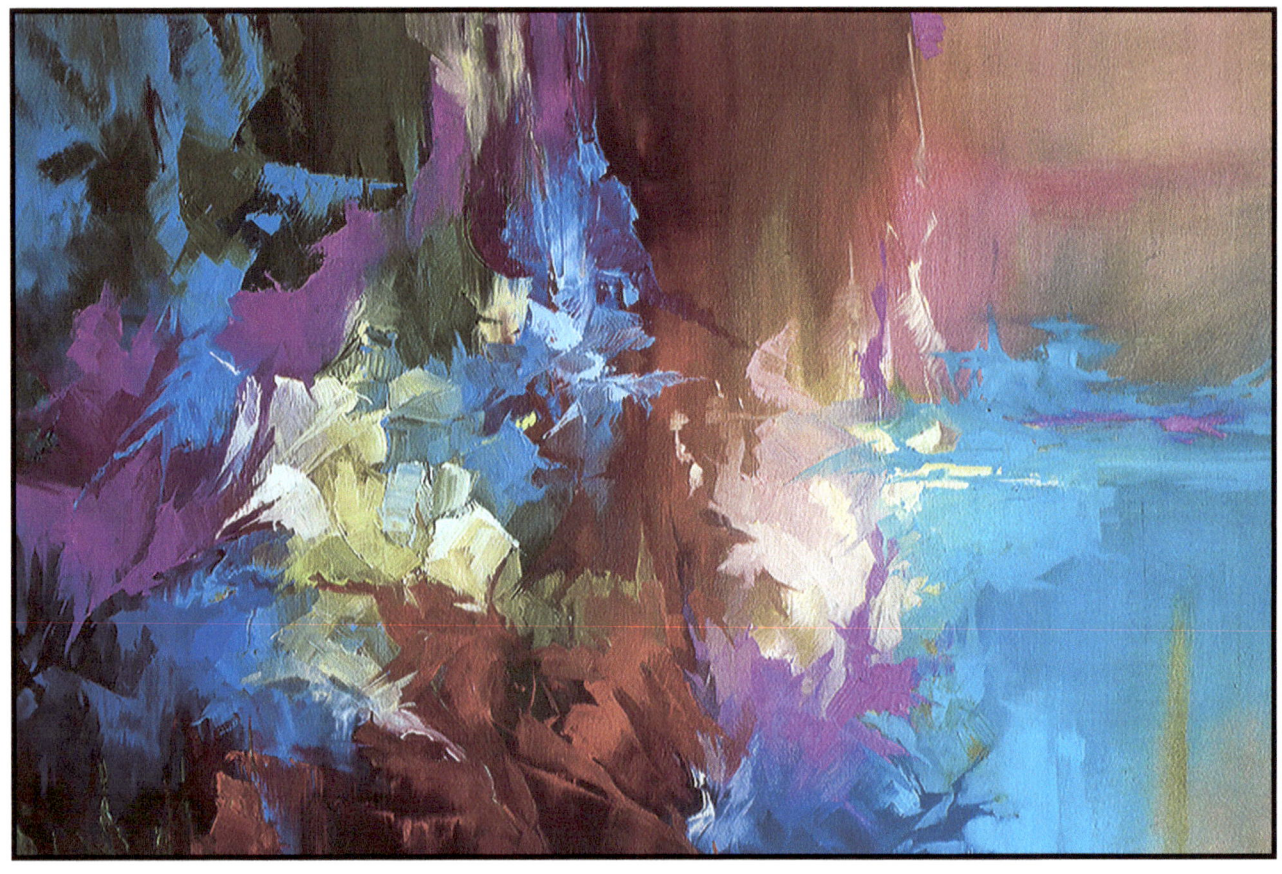

"On the Pond"
36" x 24" - Oil on Canvas
2011

"Art is the only way to run away without leaving home."
Twyla Tharp

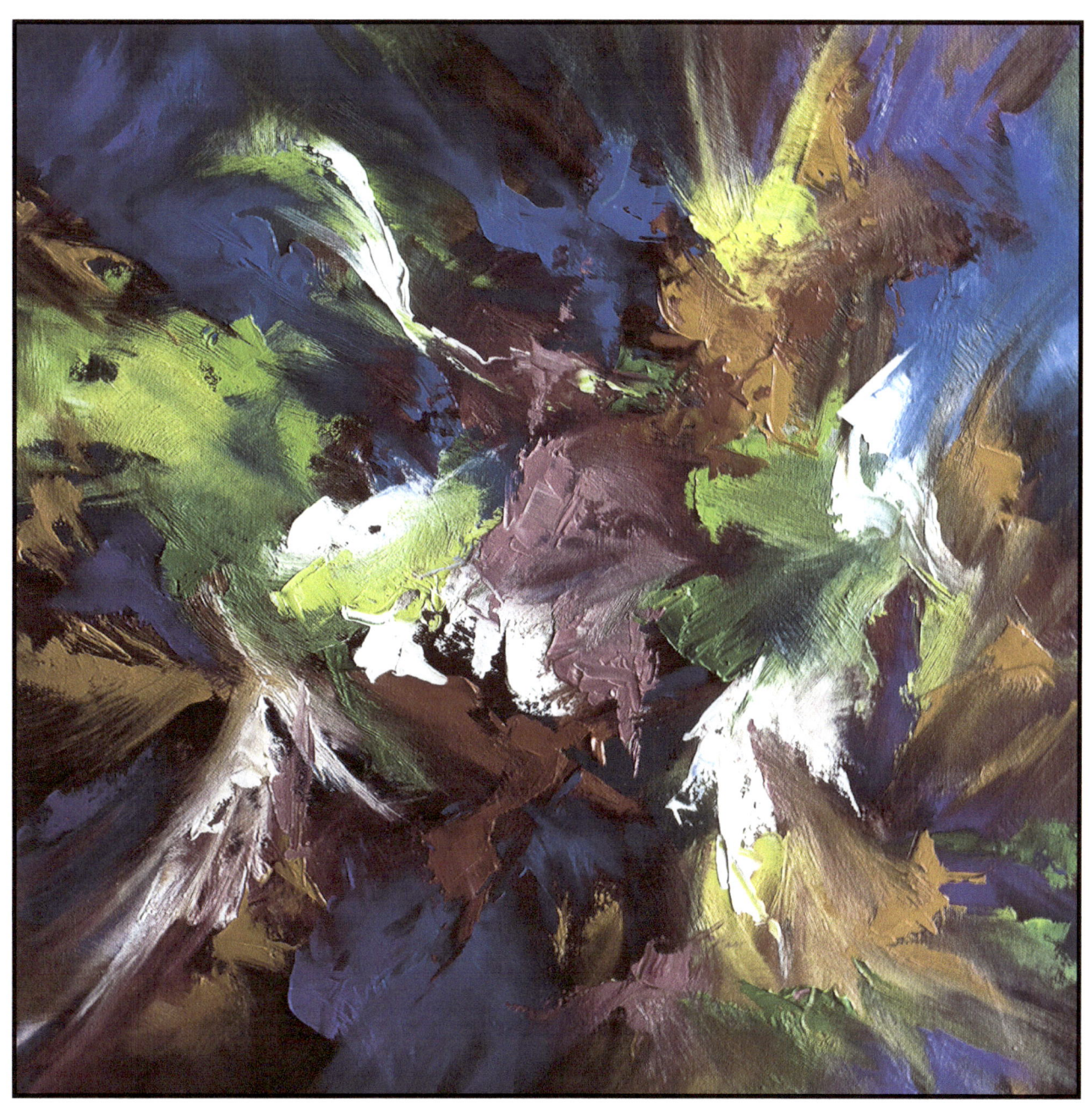

"The Dance"
18" x 18" - Oil on Canvas
2011

INNER LANDSCAPES

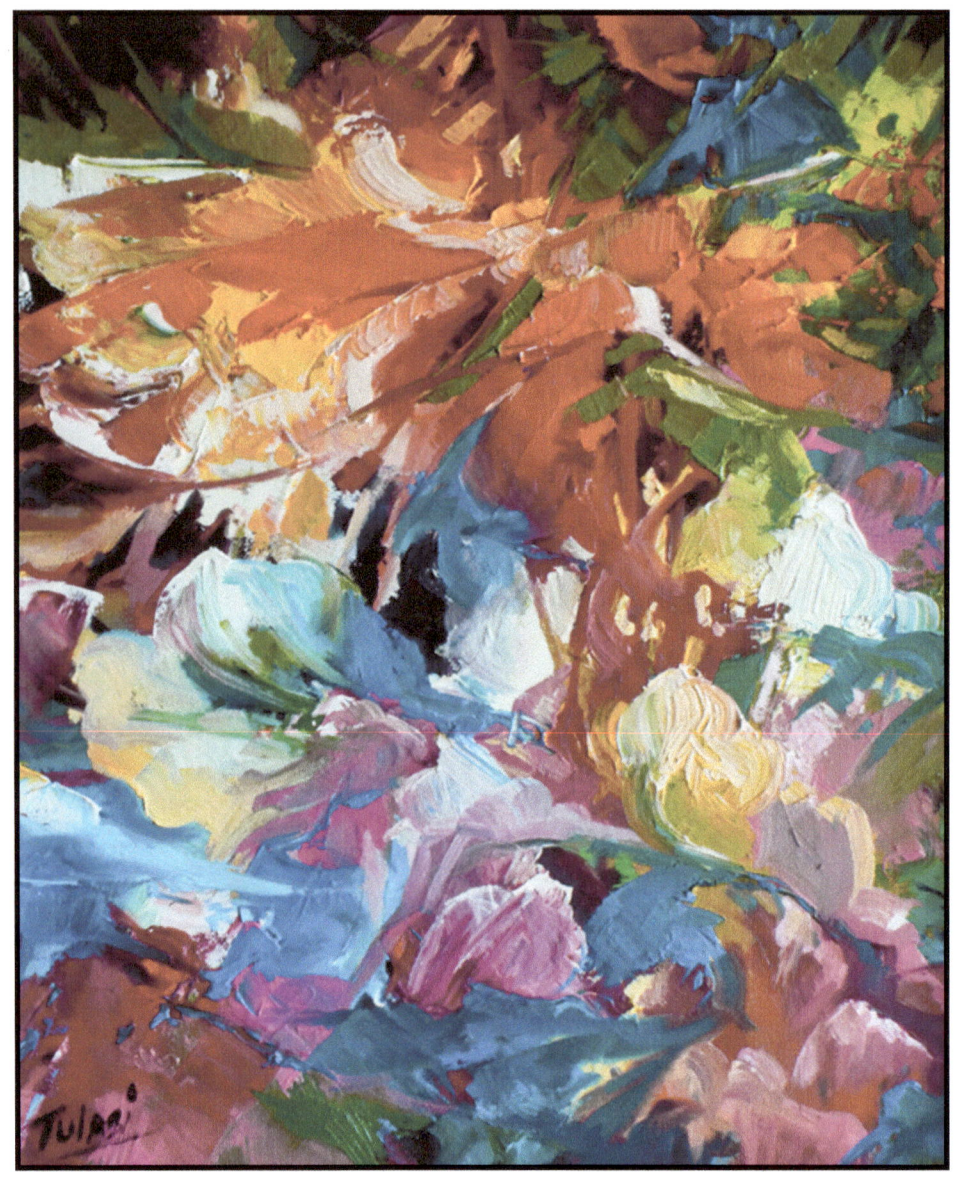

"Printemps"
12" x 16" - Oil on Canvas
2011

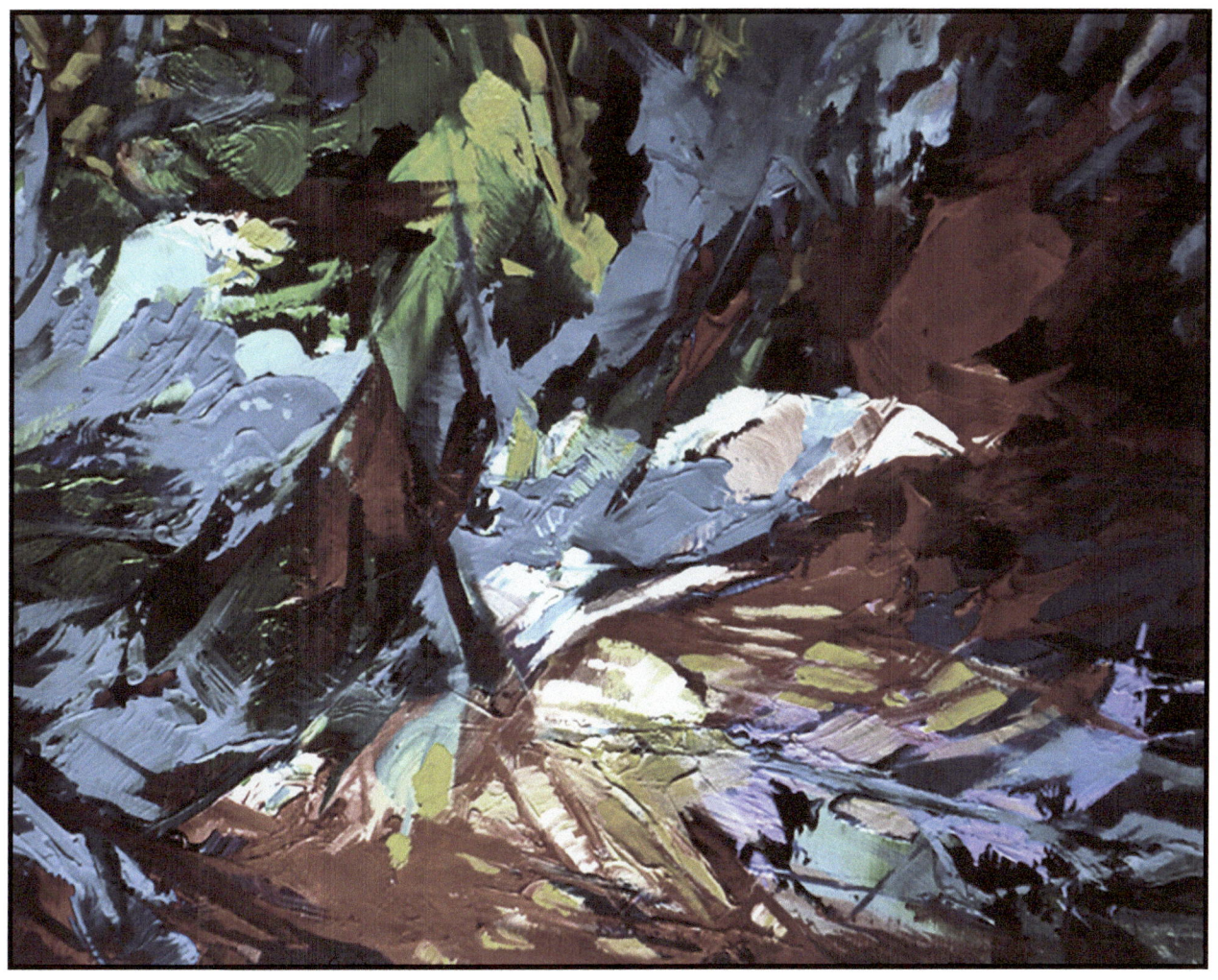

"Riverbed"
16" x 12" - Oil on Canvas
2011

"Creativity is allowing yourself to make mistakes.
Art is knowing which ones to keep."
Scott Adams

INNER LANDSCAPES

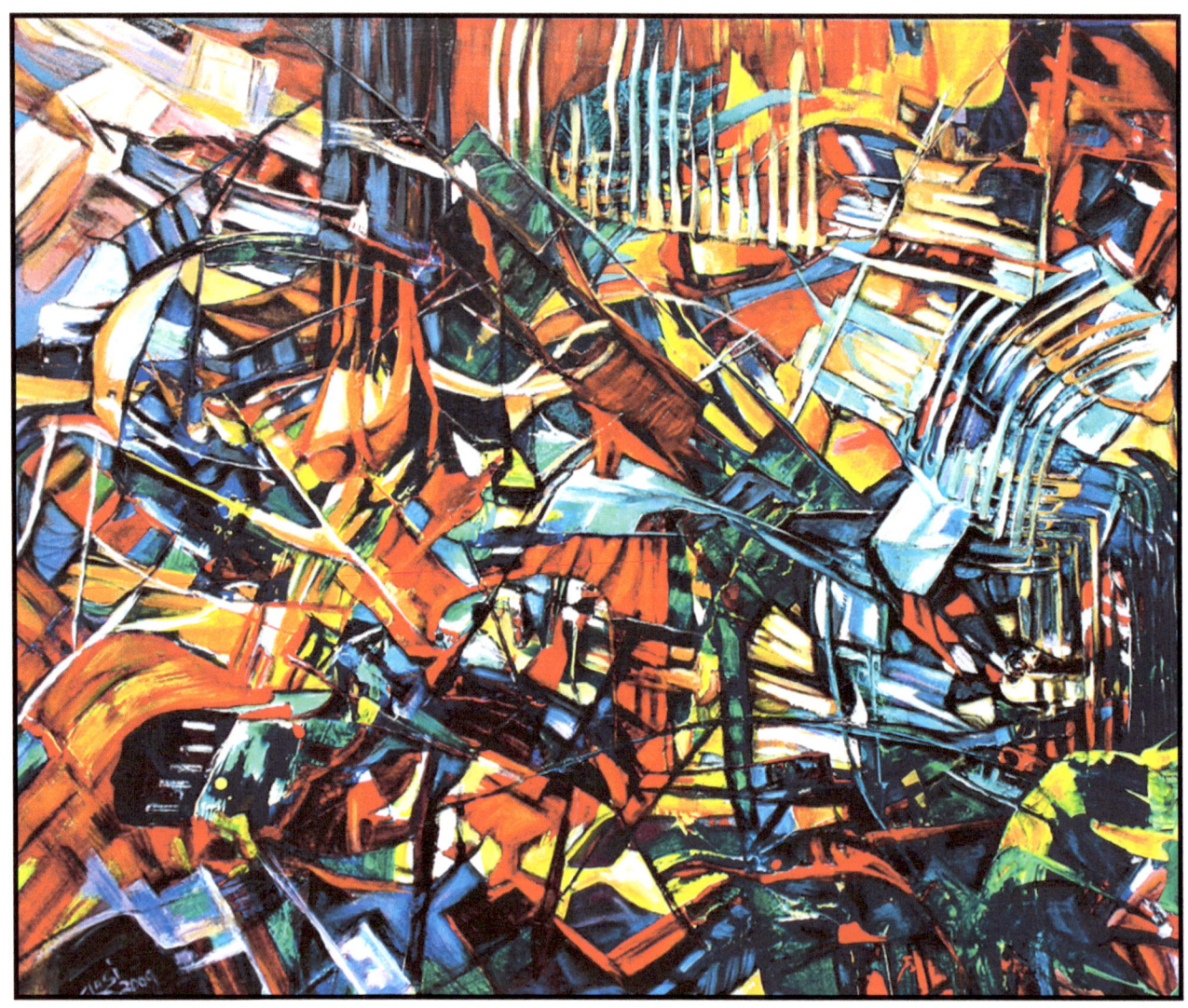

"Urban Force"
36" x 24" - Acrylic on Canvas
2009

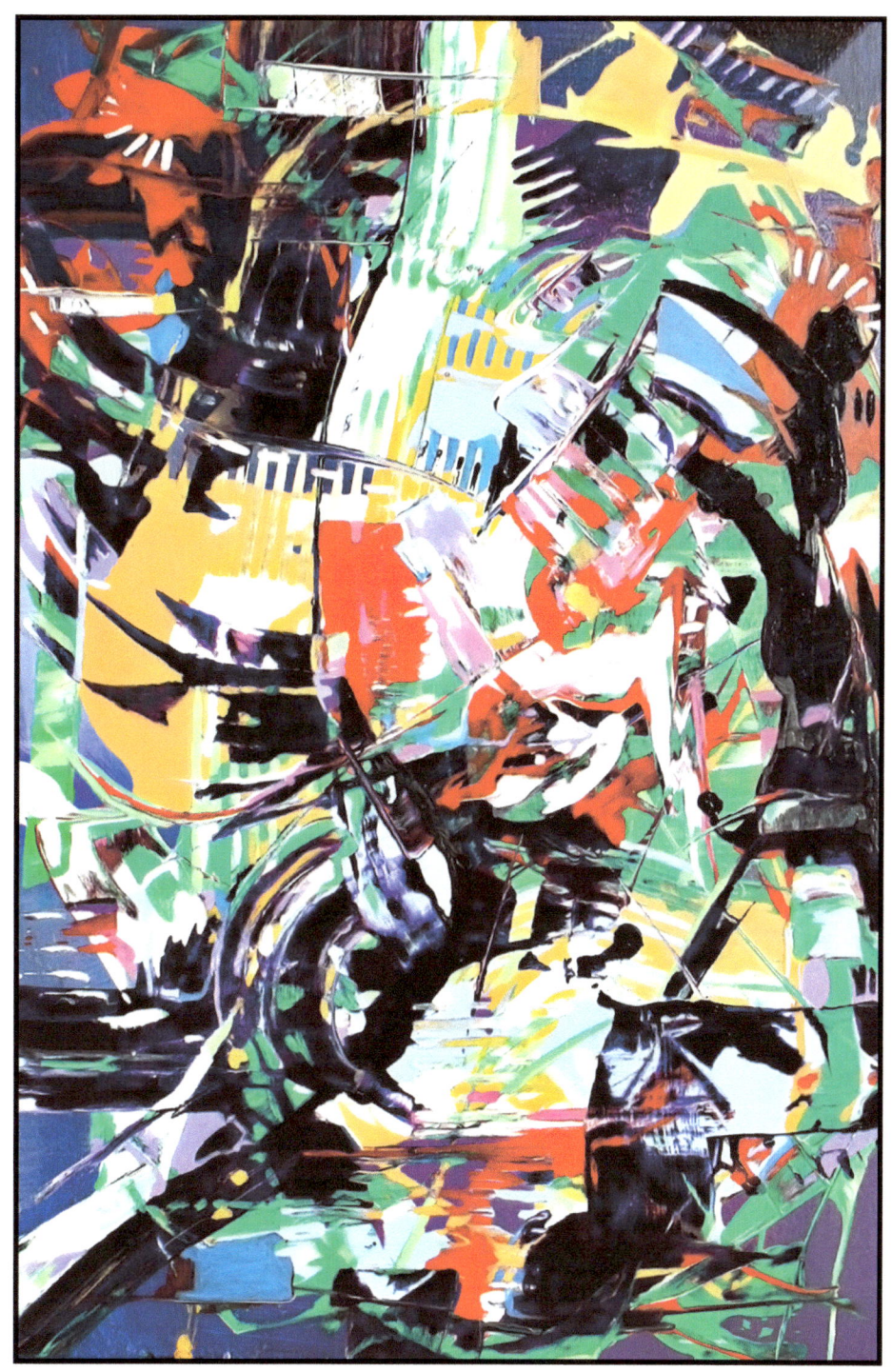

"Moving Shadows"
24" x 36" - Oil on Canvas
2009

INNER LANDSCAPES

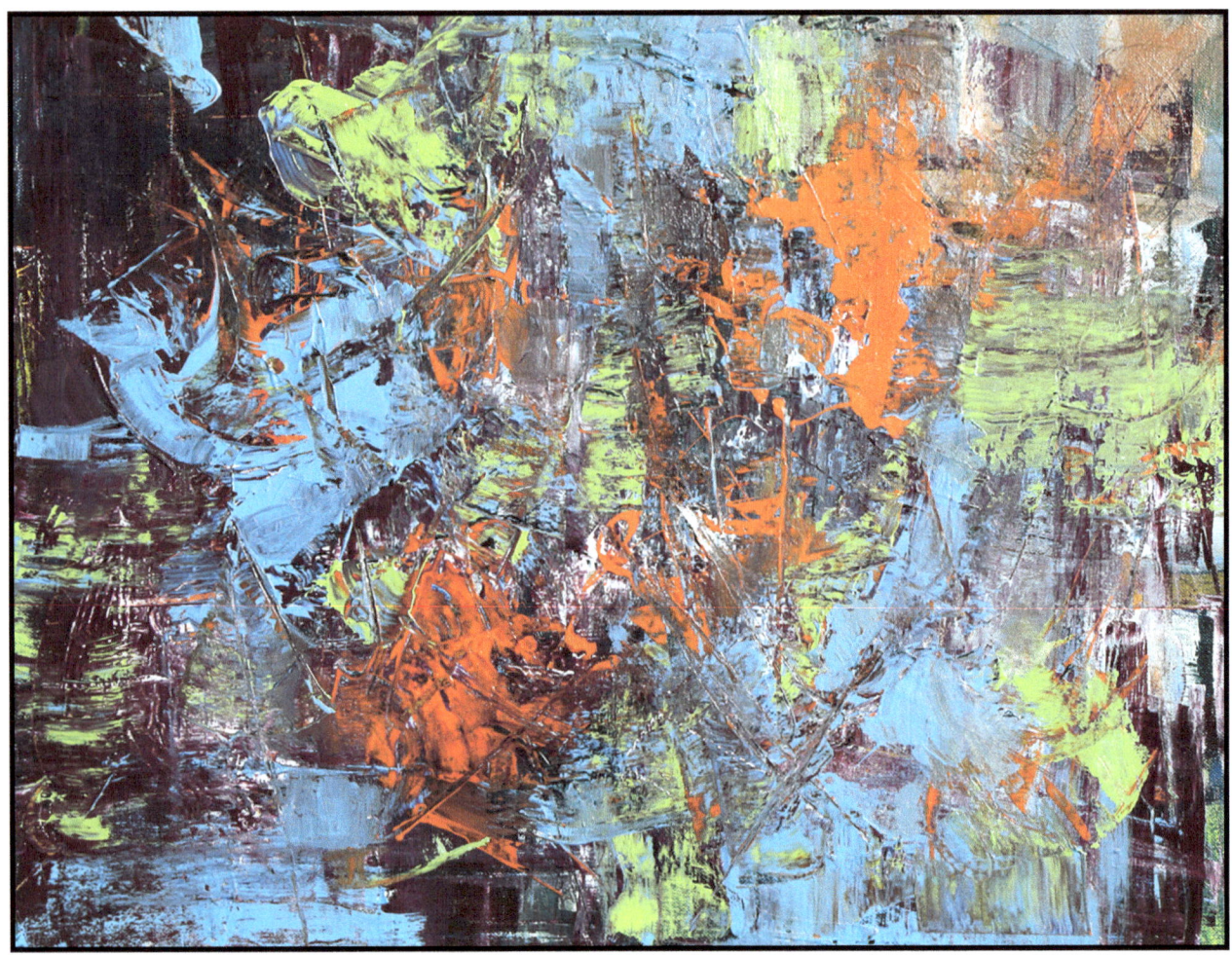

"The Wall"
24" x 18" - Oil on Board
2010

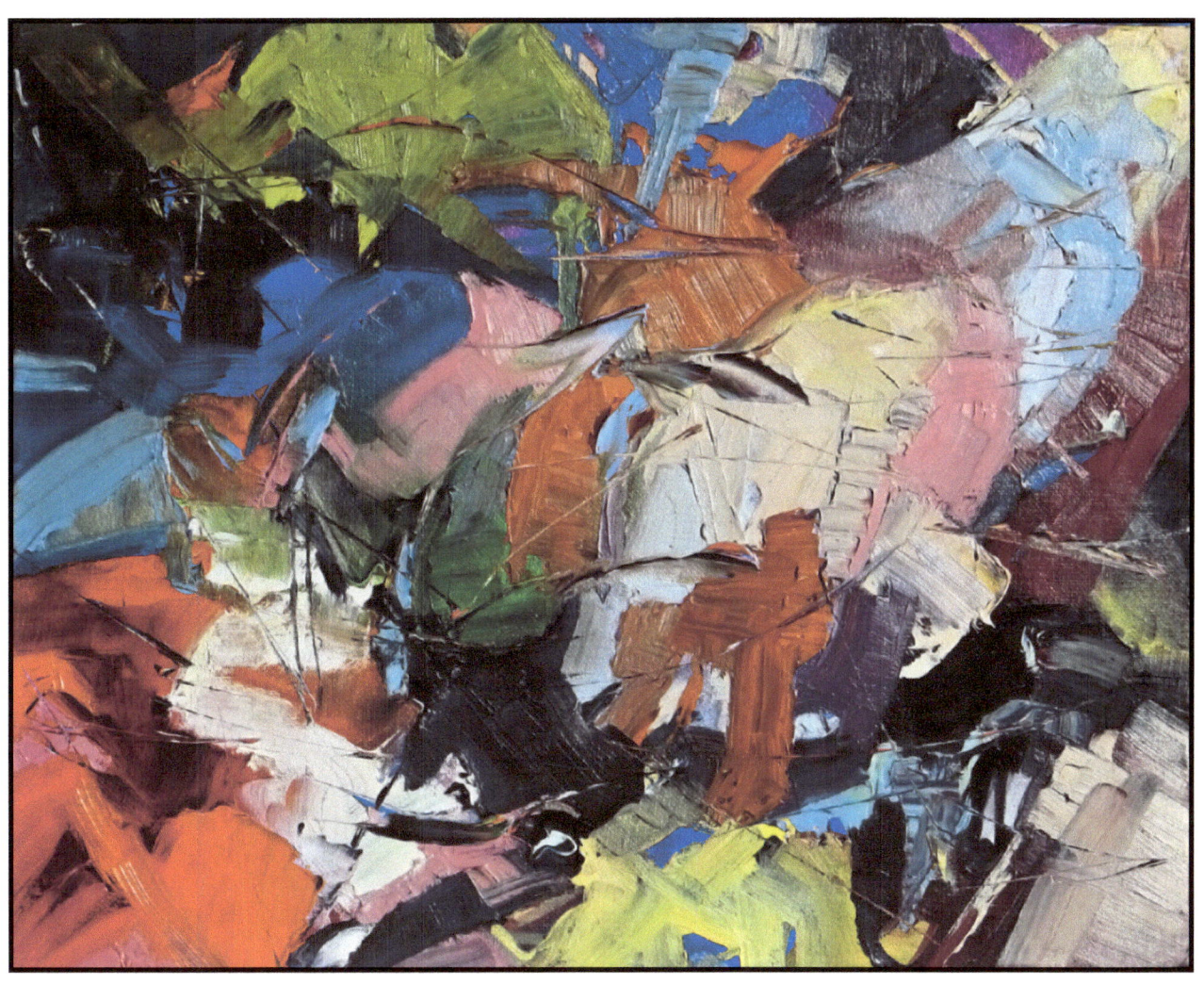

"Carnival"
30" x 24" - Oil on Canvas
2009

INNER LANDSCAPES

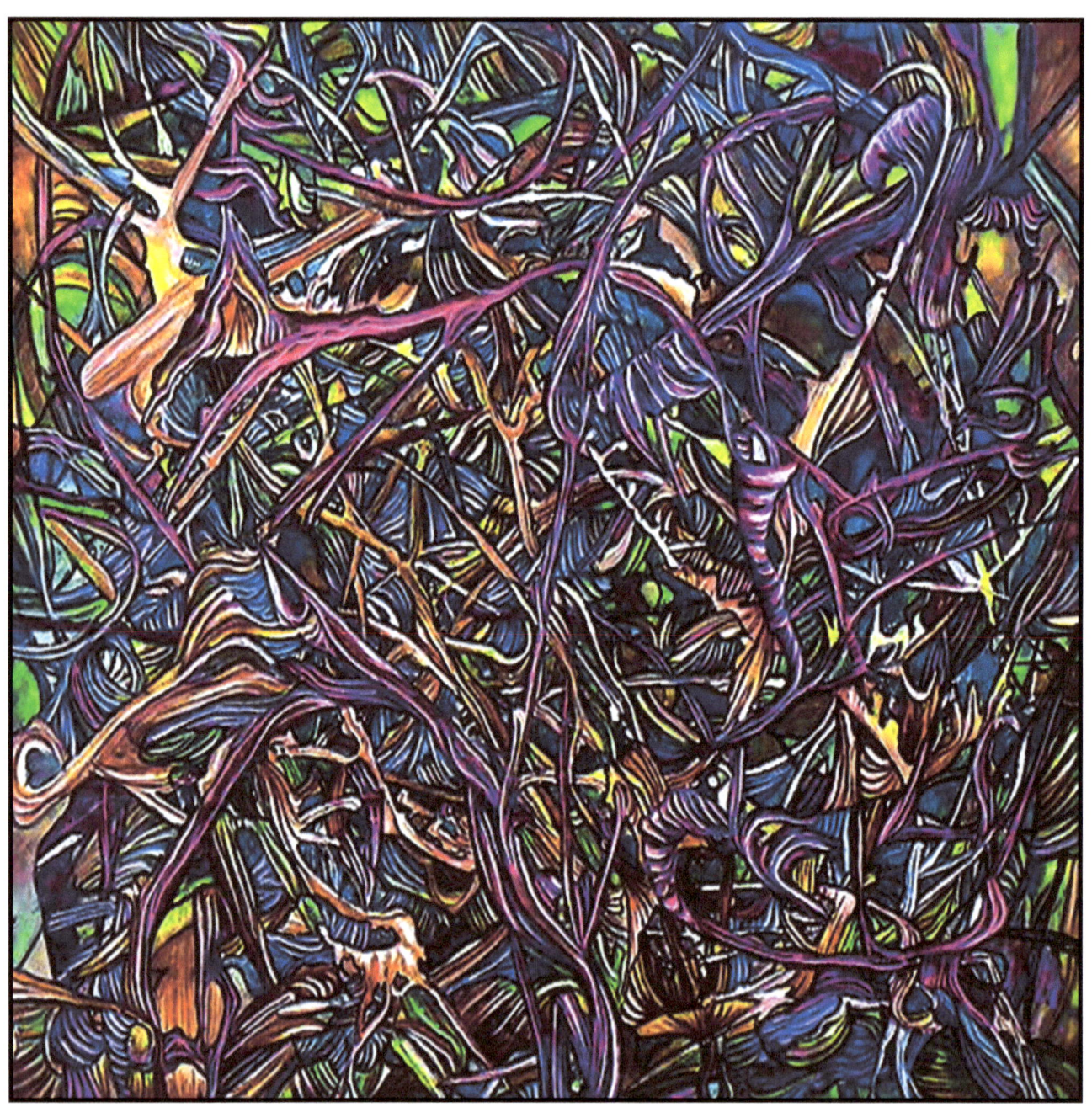

"Briar Patch"
30" x 24" - Oil on Canvas
2009

Tulasi Zimmer

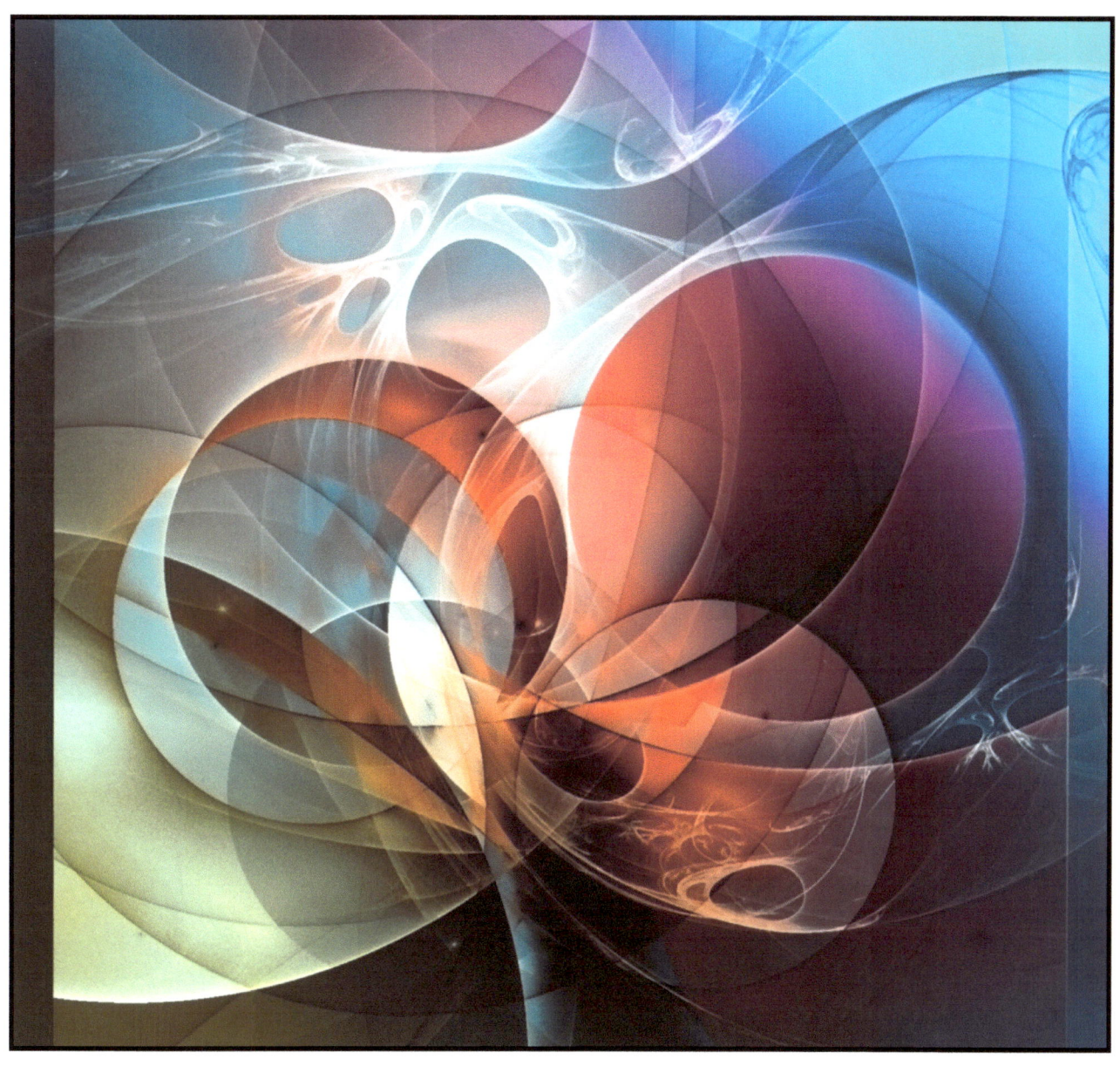

"Light Breeze"
Digital Print
2013

"An artist never really finishes his work,
he merely abandons it."
Paul Valery

INNER LANDSCAPES

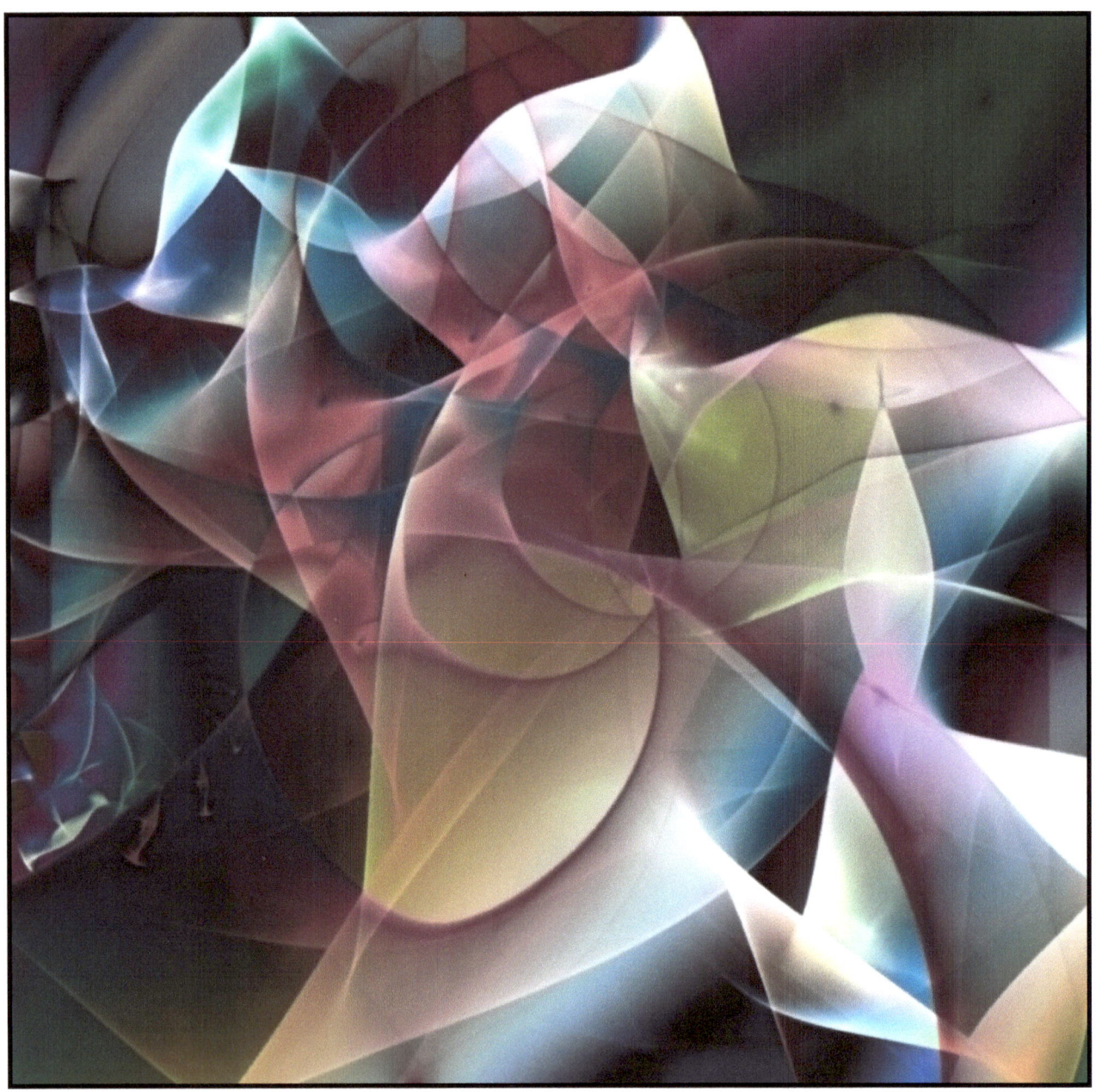

"Roll With It"
Digital Print
2013

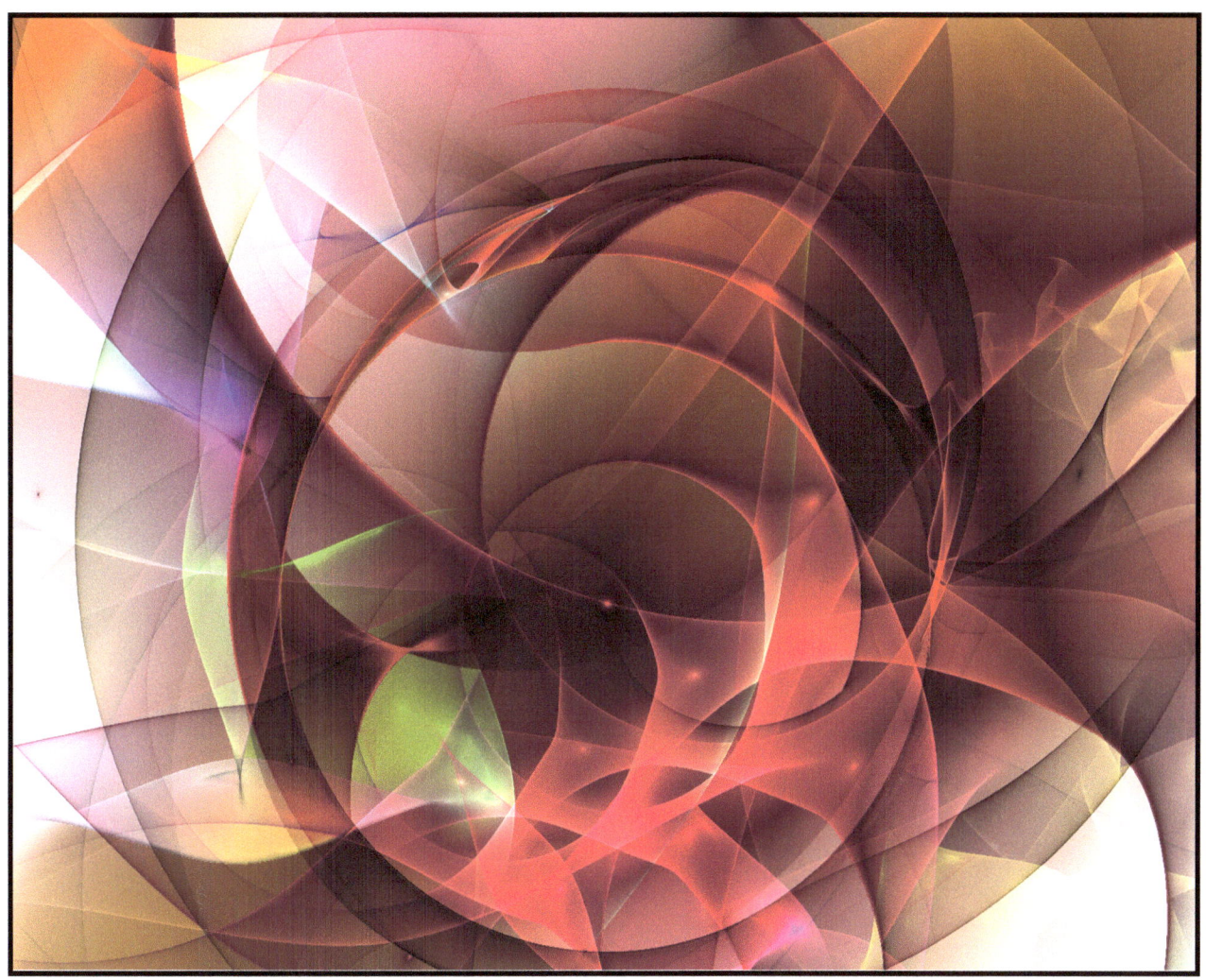

"Pinwheel"
Digital Print
2013

"Art, like morality, consists in
drawing the line somewhere."
Gilbert K. Chesterton

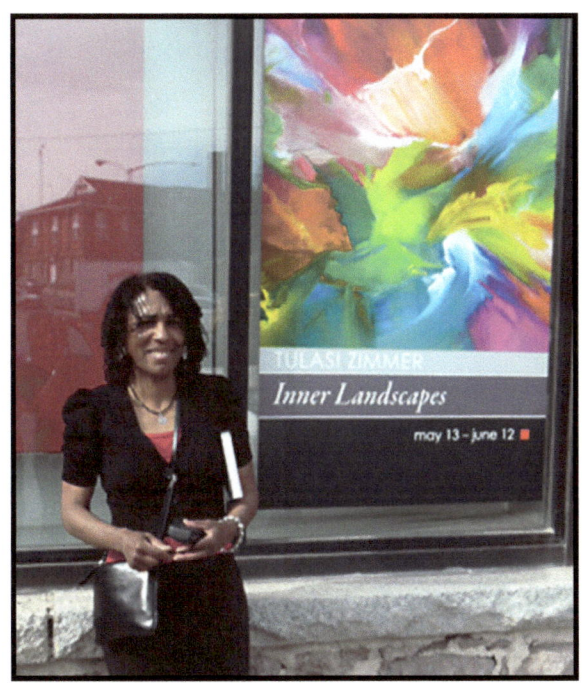

Tulasi (tul-see) Zimmer is a mid-career professional artist and educator. She grew up in Columbus, Ohio. and earned a Bachelor of Fine Arts degree (BFA) from The Ohio State University and a Master of Fine Arts degree (MFA) from Miami University of Ohio in painting, drawing, and art history. Tulasi's professional art career began when she was still in high school and includes experience as an illustrator; graphic designer; web developer; multimedia producer and publisher; computer animator; stained glass artist; fiber artist; and arts education administrator. She has created art and design for major corporations, publishers, State government, advertising agencies, institutions of higher education, and the private sector. Tulasi is an award winning oil painter and has received several national and regional awards, gallery representation in New York City, and her art work belongs to public and private collections around the world.

www.ingramcontent.com/pod-product-compliance
Lightning Source LLC
Chambersburg PA
CBHW050434180526
45159CB00006B/2528